Clark and Cleo's Clouds

by Elizabeth Bennett
illustrated by Kelly Kennedy

SCHOLASTIC INC.

New York • Toronto • London • Auckland • Sydney
Mexico City • New Delhi • Hong Kong • Buenos Aires

Designed by Maria Lilja
ISBN-13: 978-0-439-88468-6 • ISBN-10: 0-439-88468-3
Copyright © 2006 by Scholastic Inc.
All rights reserved. Printed in China.

First printing, December 2006

12 11 10 9 8 7 6 5 4 3   7 8 9 10 11/0

One day, **Clark** and his sister, **Cleo**, went to **Clovis** Park.

They **climbed** a hill and had a picnic **close** to a pretty lake.

Clark and **Cleo** thought the **clam** chowder was especially delicious!

After a while, a **cluster** of **clouds cluttered**
the **clear** sky.

"Guess what I see," said **Clark**, staring up at the **clouds**. "Here is a **clue**: He has a round nose and **clomps** around in huge shoes."

Phonics Fact

Sometimes the *cl* can come in the middle of a word, as in **exclaimed**.

"You see a **clown**!" said **Cleo**.
"Very **clever**!" exclaimed **Clark**.

Another **cluster** of **clouds** appeared.
"Guess what I see," said **Cleo**. "Here is a **clue**:
You hang them up in a **closet**."

"You see **clothes**!" said **Clark**.
"Very **clever**!" exclaimed Cleo.

Another **cluster** of **clouds** appeared.
"Guess what I see," said **Clark**. "Here is
a **clue**: If you find one in a **clump** of grass,
you will have good luck."

"You see a four-leaf **clover!**" said **Cleo**.
"Very **clever!**" exclaimed **Clark**.

Another **cluster** of **clouds** appeared.
"Guess what I see," said **Cleo**. "Here is a **clue**:
She **claps** when we **clean** our rooms."

"You see Mom!" said **Clark** with a giggle.
"Very **clever**!" exclaimed Cleo.

"Hey, Mom is pointing to a **cloud clock**.
I think she wants us to **close** up our picnic
basket and come home," **Cleo** told **Clark**.
So they did!

CL Riddles

Listen to the riddles. Then match each riddle with the right *cl* word from the box.

Word Box

clam	clown	clap	clover	close
clean	clue	climb	clock	clothes

1. You do this with your hands at the end of a play.

2. This sea creature lives in a shell.

3. It is the opposite of *dirty*.

4. It is the opposite of *open*.

5. You wear them every day.

6. You look at this to find out the time.

7. At the circus, he makes you laugh.

8. You do this to get to the top of the stairs.

9. You use this to solve a mystery.

10. If you find one with four-leaves, it will bring you luck.

CL Cheer

Hooray for *c-l*, the best sound around!

Let's holler *c-l* words all over town!

There's **cliff** and **clash** to name a few,

Clown and **clog** and **cloud** and **clue**.

There's **clock** and **club** to shout out loud,

Clean and **clang** and **clothes** and **cloud**!

C-l, c-l, **clap** and cheer,

For the **classiest** sound you ever will hear!

Make a list of other *cl* words. Then use them in your cheer.